SUSPENDED

SUSPENDED
© Ellen White Rook / Cathexis Northwest Press

No part of this book may be reproduced without written permission of the
publisher or author, except in reviews and articles.

First Printing: 2023

ISBN: 978-1-952869-77-6

Editing & Design by C. M. Tollefson
Cathexis Northwest Press

cathexisnorthwestpress.com

SUSPENDED

POEMS BY
ELLEN WHITE ROOK

Cathexis Northwest Press

For many years, I was suspended in a painful place: I wanted to write, but my confidence had disappeared. Five years ago, I ran into an old friend and fellow poet, Susan Riback. She invited me to a meeting of the Evergreen Poetry Workshop, a peer group that met monthly in a nearby arboretum. Although I was surprised by her conviction that I would be able to contribute, by the end of the first gathering, I was excited to find myself rediscovering the challenge of poetry and exploring how the fragile, brilliant moments of our lives can be suspended in the space of a page.

This collection of poems would not have been possible without the ongoing inspiration, support, and encouragement of Susan, the members of the Evergreen Poetry Workshop, and the Capital Region Poet's Workshop. I am deeply grateful to these brilliant writers, constructive readers, and dear friends.

Dwell. Linger. Stay.
　　　　–Baron Wormser

Table of Contents

Long light day	3
Brave red	5
Internal sutures	6
After harvest	7
Sparrows fall	8
On waking	9
Nine red lines	10
Emigrant song	11
Musica humana	13
Two(mbly) by the sea	15
Use caution	16
Heart of glass	21
Blue	22
Oh brother	24
Alone in the finite but expanding universe	25
Ruins	26
At cashel rock	27
After loss	28
Suspended	29
Thrush morning	31
New baby poem	32
	33

Long light day

at the end
>my father stopped
swallowing
but for years before
his skin peeled
ruddy patches
my mother smeared
with orange unguent

his limbs increasingly
>contracted
towards a stiff heap
all angles awkward
like driftwood piled
on a harsh
hot day
for midnight fire
his neck bent
as if broken

my father stopped
>speaking
the last few words
extinguished
thank you
dear

he stopped looking
>at anything anyone else
could see
eyes still
deep forest dark
red brown green
flecked with gold

when he stopped
>breathing
and was carried away
in a black SUV
my brother followed
to the crematorium
afraid he would be mislaid
between death

        and the ritual
        end

today I am making
        a summer fire
        first a stone ring to contain
        branches then twigs
        paper crumpled
        in a pyramid
        an offering
        of smoke and light
        for the too-hot day
        beside the pyre
        a rusted pail
        of cool water

I am thinking
        about the unstoppable
        how a spark consumes
        dry things
        how water
        swallows fire

there is gold
        in the sun's flash
        on green

there is gold
        under the earth
        in a box
        of ash

BRAVE RED

                    In this country
there is no minister for loneliness.
We make do with general anxiety.
The wind, loose, plucks
the last pinecones and builds
horizontal crowns across the snow.
After this year of masking
breath and fingers pressed
against glass walls, houseplants
are overgrown from too much care:
Ivies overthrow terracotta
and aloe spikes weave
through jades.
                    An amaryllis
that hasn't bloomed in years,
this week leapt a green arc from its nest
of tiny stones. The thumb-bud aims
precisely where the sun comes up
even though I turn the pot
each morning, and some days,
the sky stays winter pale.
The red sepals unfold
precisely the shade
of that last lipstick smile.

Internal Sutures

I pull thread
once invisible
now tipped
rigid
cruel
and useless
as the aglet
on a snapped shoelace

It pokes opaque
through the healing
seam

Fibers weep
and stick to skin

So much fluff

Once marrow knew
how to navigate stars
Soles pounded through
sod and coal
to the earth's ripe core

It was not just tension
that made
movement speech
but sense spoke name
and recognized
the world

As it all
unravels
assembly reveals
pieces laid
to rocking
flat
Fine white threads
that look like clouds
strain to find
forever

AFTER HARVEST

As if you wintered in
a seasonless resort
I press maple leaves between
wax paper
red yellow orange
I iron hands of leather oak
I parcel acorns
their empty caps
and whirligigs

In winter I'll fold
white paper
three times
and with tiny scissors
fabricate
the plates and needles
of flake

I'll send the tiny squares
and cut-out hearts so you can
toss them in the air

For your children
who play
in rivers
of fire
pain
forgetfulness
wailing
and boundary

Who hide-and-seek
in corners
tangle in dust
fallen lashes
instars and broken
glow

Send me their pictures

I'll carry them in the daisy pocket
of my summer apron

SPARROWS FALL

I asked her if she remembered when Oklahoma came to Connecticut, dust covering the sun, leaving grasslands' parched thirst on windows, roads, and sheets snapping on the line.

She did not, though it was front page news: millions of tons of topsoil storming, millions of dollars of fertilizer wind-stolen from bare fields, small birds flung back to earth.

It happened again, and again, until drought ended in 1939.

It may have been unremarkable to a five-year-old.

She might have thought the yellow curtain was a foggy haze, the shore moved inland for the day, with dust so fine it would not settle until utter calm.

She did not recall the smell or taste, but this summer, when wildfires brought a damaged transparency to the sky, when the sun was a wild penny quavering, my tongue understood.

This is the bite a child might overlook.

Scent hung in the under places: steep ravines and hollowed cliffs.

It lingered at the riverbank.

Like the taste of some dead living thing, it seemed to bite through sunset's glory and the perforated night.

I am hollowed hard with memories of what we have ignored: gone bees, migrations confused, the earth upended, moving where it does not belong.

This was the second summer of fires, big as nations, the planet prying our bodies awake.

To remember, never to forget, to not be a child distracted by crayons at a table.

On Waking

the oracle leaves
footprints in water that turn to ice
a winter palace
that sieves the sun

      inside
      I dream of swimming
      in a summer pond

words spoken hang
in myths
knife-silver light sits
on murky water
not a reflection but the place
between object and impression
at the edge

      in reeds
      the heron stands
      rises
      all stillness
      ready to strike

there is evidence I am here awake
that I have been moving
speaking
sometimes listening
a lined face
bones that have lost their boneness
dust whispered into clouds

      the water I slip into is neither hot nor cold
      alive with frogs and weeds and slim grey fish
      I am noiseless as a faraway stone

the heron cries
one slender leg bent
about to breathe
dive
about to kill
the seam between
waking and dreaming
unspeakable

      the pond perfumes my hair

NINE RED LINES

> *Nine red lines on a stone flake found in a South African cave may be the earliest known drawing made by Homo sapiens.*
> New York Times, September 13, 2018

-one-

    my hand draws down
pulling the root
out of the sky

-two-

              down
    down
down
all
caught
and catching
becoming
rain
tears
a palm-sized
rock bouldered
into my heavy
hand

-three -

    limbless trunks
straight unbound
something emerges
from in between
but it is the space between
not what embraces
that severs the beginning
slashes the curve of heart
the core of all

-four-

yet unstable
like wind
        palms joined
hide
something
more than just one and other
brings
more
more than what will fly apart

-five-

              a whole of itself
nothing to be done
undoing

-six-

        someone brought stories
of hot days and nights so cold
it was how our bones
lay
when they found us

-seven-

in what we were hiding from
riddles
my hands tire
from carrying
from
talking
around the same
old story

-eight-

the sun
a line where day starts and ends
where the moon turns
to a humped curve
everything
scraped in
collected

-nine-

                    blood
rests
on sharpness
knowing
complete beginning
birth blood
word
wet
greasy
earth joins voice
touches
vision
in glorious
exclamation

Emigrant song

> *Go back home*
> Popular Saying (United States)

if I walk
if my mother walks
if her mother walks
    will I ever feel other than
    an anxious guest
if one could be a guest
    where walls fail
    to fields
    and sunrise
    incises space with
    black tree
    trunks
if I follow
    and find a river
    that might touch
    the tide
    of my departure
    will it follow
    my mother's
    handled cup
    her mother's fingers
    the scrubbed steps
    leading to
    declaration
    of intent
if I speak
if my mother speaks
if her mother speaks
    forgotten consonants
    with our red
    hands and cracked bones
if cognate brooms
    land nowhere
    to sweep strongbox
    certificates
    will roots
    recognize the
    cadence

        or correct
        the rhythm
        join
        the aspen's trembling
        metronome
when all the stars
        are shadows
        and misremembered
        planets percolate
        silver signs
        overgrown by bark or rusted
        dull or lost
        on wind felled
        trunks
when there is no
        border
between breath
        and sleep
        our headstones
        tipped
        against the weeds
        will home be
        home

MUSICA HUMANA

in the far from dawn
dark
        an unruly bird wakes
                    tumbles rock
consonants
            sucks the warm blanket
from my shoulders
               a handful of kosher salt
       cutting the naked soles
of dream

insistent impediment to sleep

            yet the feeder is moonless
seeds and suet star dark
      the noisy bird should be deep
            in arbor vitae
        hedge
head tucked asleep not
           calling out
unanswered

I wonder what has roused this wild
thrashing sing
          and find

featherless
      cacophony
beside me
      a husband bird
          making a murder
              of vocal
chords

the percussion hungers melody
      pulse and improvisation trills
          towards beauty

    too early
        I rest
    in the chirrup of the spheres until
the return to sleep becomes

the even more beautiful sing

Two(mbly) the Sea

~ I ~

Out there
        the words of my father
        expire
and sink
                            What the sun left on waves after

                                      it sunk
                                    spun frippery

                Mask plaster stuck to their faces like bones or broken toys

Citrus
            or stone
       fruit
            lemon or more succulent
                              Hello

                                Is something out there?

Jealousy makes no waves
no logic but after dark steals deep

                                      Come to me

make a net of quiet
                   and forgiveness

Islands and shores

                                Children play too hard
                     The wind
      cuts them
                                  into shovels and pails

Stories of rectangular rafts
                          run aground

One captures the rest

Tides well

                                          Forensic

                                                                                 myth
unique
          fingers print

                                                                Sadness without regret
                          grit and
       salt

            The illusion of stillness

Where   where   where
                              shadow

                      wood

                                                                       bone

~II~

You
cannot
erase every
trace
or the little
cries of big
birds
The poem
speaks to what is
not there
an object
with its
public
private attributes
words
trucked in
barefoot
exposed
to
clouds on a
golden
splendidness
The sea has
no one
looking
out down across
An object has attributes
which we could call
fields
or qualities
The ease of
the sea is not
the sea
even
when the lines are azure
rough
and
clear

~III~

A poem to the sea is not the sea
The sea is a symbol of itself

It is not an eloquent reflection
or the tossing
of flotsam and jetsam
or moving
or muddying
or deep light
dark beyond treasure
or the myriad creatures

> Once upon
> a tide I
> invented mermaids
> and costumed little
> girls
> crocheted seaweed hung
> with star skeletons and
> scallop shells

A poem to the sea is at the edge
which is torn against a long silver rule that arcs
when you hold it like a sword
inviting advance

The paper tears wide open swathes
broadside shore to land on
when the tide is low

> Their tails were
> iridescent pink and blue
> They were my poems to the sea

It never disappears entirely
framed or rolled
ribbon tied

> They wore small crowns
> they made
> crumpling silver
> foil around cardboard

Poem to the sea
has no code
to decode

There is no color intermediate
to green
and horizontal
to violet

                              They grew their dreams in slipper shells
                                            hair bobbed and shone
                                             on days they floated
                                                  and were found
                                                         by sun

The poem is a symbol of itself
a gesture sand makes in an array
They do not exist without the other

                                                     Waves comb
                                                      sea snarls
                                              The little mermaids
                                              dance slipper shells
                                           We write poems the sea
                                              reads as it washes
                                                     even when
                                         we are picked clean like
                                                  lead and chalk

The stain of the sea is not the sea
is not the poem of the sea
The sea reads
in its own rinse and rise
with epic ease

Use Caution

Between Brunswick and Bath
rain collects beside the beaten road
slaps against the cove's skyward-facing palms
disturbs the ditches' slim, silver fingers

Rain collects beneath bridges where it doesn't fall

I worry I will be transfixed by these liquid beginnings
which will not grow into anything that breathes
or swims

The unthreaded downpour pricks and overspills
my drowned coat and never sews
the old season done

Nothing is hard as spring
the dark machine that returns
the winter-weak goldfinch to a wire
swinging in the rain

Is there is a seed I might nurture
in my hard self
the way bones cultivate
marrow?

Daylight blares
on grey

Heart of Glass

I want
an explanation
for why my heart seems
so opaque
dense and smooth
to the touch
like windshield glass
yet meant to be transparent
a means to move tender
and knowing
through the world

*

wind shakes the tallest pines
pollen banners swirl
and hang the shadow
of an empty mountain

settles yellow-green

*

can we see clarity
without confusion's canvas?

can we discern word
without space?

*

as I travel
leftover rain
quivers in the corner
where wipers can't reach
pushes the drops to green-rimmed
exclamations
lines that squirm
to letters maybe
words

cool to the fingertips

hard

heart tempered
to be safely breakable

how
to collect the jagged pieces?

how to fit them back together
into something clear?

*

on a snake-black line
a robin perches
breast unmuted
impossible orange

*

the juggling wind
smears promises
blood
a handful of pollen

nothing wipes clean

*

I want to believe
some truth can be
deciphered
in the unraveling corner
and loved
by my blind
fingers

BLUE

On reading Eavan Boland

sweaty from the walk that started grey
swarmed with damp risen
from rain-shadowed road
and ended blazing
backlit trees dulled to black
fluffed clouds stranded

on the blue couch I am happy reading
silent drapes move abruptly as if rattling
sun blinds the page just a little
so blue suffuses it as well

I am happy reading
as if sitting with my sister
borders invisible as night
light and water resting
in my breathing
in my stars
in my blue

OH BROTHER

Through the window in your front door
I see the pile of unopened mail
sliding from beneath the mail slot
around the corner to the living room
where a rocking chair is baffled
with log cabin quilts
Petals from the Christmas cactus
skitter on the hardwood floor
red wrinkled to the palest brown
How long ago did it bloom?

I wanted to tell you I walked
in the park we had talked of going to
near the old house but closer to the river
through stone gates
up and down the sculpted hills

There were swathes of blue Siberian Squill
pushing against the noisy leaves
and at the overlook I could see
a dozen swans swimming upriver
parallel to the Seekonk's shore
There was a man dozing on the bench
where I wanted to sit down
the way we used to rest
I would eat an apple
You would smoke a cigarette

It would not have changed anything
but I should have brought you coffee
or a pot of pansies
their faces cheerful
but bruised

ALONE IN THE FINITE BUT EXPANDING UNIVERSE

when stars and night reverse
we enter the black mouth
slow muscles propel
our bodies
down gravity's
gullet

when stars and day reverse
blue stays
and clouds if there are clouds
are clouds

last night's
dreams seem preposterous
as a fanciful quilt
with stories painted
between planes
of light

in this
monochromatic inversion
Cassiopeia stumbles
from the throne
her cape unfurls
and masks
the legend
of her humiliated
spine

because we cannot help
but make another story
even in the absence
of infinity

what I offered to the sky
gone

distance makes everything small
but pain
and I am smaller
than darkness
severed

Ruins

I am so far from anywhere
yet alongside my walking
a low stone wall meanders
the kind to use up stumbling stones
too low to hold a sheep or cow
just tall enough to say
this is the field I'll plant someday
this is the edge of me

a dooryard runs violets out to the path
drifts of round heart leaves
white petals with black freckles
and the ordinary purple
and I can smell lilacs before I see
their dark panicles guarding the stone corner
where there used to be a house
which has collapsed into its own foundation
weathered boards and knobless doors askew
half-hidden by oak leaves and soil
fine as dust but thick enough for weeds
to grow and almost hide glass shards

they didn't live here long
not long enough for anyone to build a road
or draw the small house on a map
or set their names in village history

a plain yellow butterfly
finds the honey scent of flowers
and under waves of briars newly leaved
I spy the raft roof of a chicken coop
sinking into the afternoon

AT CASHEL ROCK

My sister slept on Cashel rock
with her best friend
It was in the days before cell phones
They missed the tour bus call
There was no one to call
and nowhere to go
They could not remember how they came
The only lights were planets
and summer's falling stars

All quiet
cows milked
and returned to sheds
Sheep ceased to bleat
There was only rock
limestone jagged huge
thrust like anger on bucolic fields
and built on that ruggedness
stone floors and roofless halls
the empty-arched cathedral
overwhelmed the seat of kings
a place where prayer has been accomplished
and abandoned
surrounded by graves

As in a fairy tale
they slept on stone
When morning fell with fog
they woke with laces tight
wet and knotted hard
Red-wrinkled creases fixed like wires
between their skin and bones
They stretched like giants
asleep a thousand years

Our people come from near this rock
They must have passed it on the road to market
and on that last journey to the ship that took them here
They might have looked at it the way
I see the abandoned slaughterhouse
beside the highway
defunct unusable but still
unyielding hard
a thick-walled ruin that smells
of dust and fire and blood

After loss

Let me
tell you
what I found
jay feather
blue black gray
a stone
from a crushed driveway
squared
like a fortification
the paper fortune-teller
fallen from a child's notebook
I fly the wings
and peel open
the final triangle
in block letters
no when only
a season could
answer
the question

I found the scissors
that were never lost
they were pinking
shears and every heart
had a rick rack
battlement

I found the cookbook
sticky brown with batter
instructions stuck
to paper words

When I dug
I found my tendon
trowel-arm sore
I found ash under
every nail

The upside-down clock
makes nonsense
of the day
what time is it
are we there

The treasures
in my jeans pocket
trip the translucent shaft
empty of
itself like
chipmunk tunnels
and the small mountain
behind the high green
hedge in the cemetery
where they put
the sand and clay
displaced
from graves

Suspended

        this is the time of year
when I'm a root-wrapped stone
dull under weeks-old snow
as more falls in slanted
lines that layer soft
orderly ashes
pale
a poor exchange
for light

        (the empty sun
        forgot to rise
        and the morning cardinal
        at the feeder was black
        as a crow)

red
a memory of blood

green
requires transpiration
thaw

        approaching death
or just the end
all shapes
still wanting
to be born again
into this life

        (animal
        vegetable
        mineral)

sky frozen
under foot
stone wishing for sap
sap wishing
for heartwood

Thrush Morning

        before dawn's
shell-shiny
start I notice
finally
winter damage
on the neighbor's pine
the top blown
into its own branches
and hear
from within this high
dark tangle
voice
        he sings
a simple chord
two tones
or one
so rich and pure
it makes a layer
like the sound of light
enveloping
the moon
or fingers
on a soft
cheek
        this small
brown bird
offering the blossom
of almost spring
his split syrinx
captures all directions
as the egg-sun
oranges the broken tree
a dazzling parapet
overlooking
his charmed
territory

New Baby Poem

he rests
shimmering
seeming to reflect the world
but watching
restless as water
as noisy
as quiet
we hold to each other
leaf and water
resting and waiting
even though
I believed I had been lost
to bone and dust

I wish to thank the following publications where some of these poems first appeared:

Anti-Heroin Chic, "Blue," "Long light day," "Ruins"
Audience Askew, "Use caution"
Barzakh Magazine, "The flute says"
Cold Mountain Review, "Thrush morning"
Hudson River Writes Guild, "After loss," "At Cashel Rock"
New Note Poetry, "Nine red lines"
New Verse News, "Brave red"
Rock and Sling, "Emigrant song"
RockPaperPoem, "Oh brother"
Rubbertop Review, "Alone in the finite but expanding universe"
Split Rock Review, "Sparrows fall"
The Banyan Review, "On Waking," "Suspended"
The Black Fork Review, "After harvest"
Tofu Arts Ink Press, "Two(mbly) the sea"
Wings of Wonder, "Musica humana"

"At Cashel Rock" is what I imagined happened when my sister was stranded at Cashel Rock over forty years ago. I recently learned that she simply walked to a Bed & Breakfast and spent a comfortable night. In 2022, Tobin's First Prize Center, the slaughterhouse mentioned in the final stanza, was demolished, leaving only an iconic smokestack that is scheduled to be taken down.

"Sparrows fall" was inspired by Timothy Egan's National Book Award winner, *The Worst Hard Time*.

"Two(mbly) the sea" responds to Cy Twombly's 1959 series *Poems to the Sea*.

Ellen White Rook is a poet and contemplative arts teacher who divides her time between upstate New York and Maine. Retired from a career as an information technology manager, she now offers writing workshops and leads retreats that combine meditation, movement, and writing. She also teaches Japanese flower arranging in the Sogetsu tradition. Ellen holds a Master of Fine Arts degree from Lindenwood University and has been twice nominated for the Pushcart Prize. *Suspended* is her first collection of poetry. She is married and has three adult daughters. To read more of her work, visit her website at ellenwhiterook.com.

Also Available from Cathexis Northwest Press:

Something To Cry About
by Robert Krantz

Suburban Hermeneutics
by Ian Cappelli

God's Love Is Very Busy
by David Seung

that one time we were almost people
by Christian Czaniecki

Fever Dream/Take Heart
by Valyntina Grenier

The Book of Night & Waking
by Clif Mason

Dead Birds of New Zealand
by Christian Czaniecki

The Weathering of Igneous Rockforms in High-Altitude Riparian Environments
by John Belk

If A Fish
by George Burns

How to Draw a Blank
by Collin Van Son

En Route
by Jesse Wolfe

sky bright psalms
by Temple Cone

Moonbird
by Henry G. Stanton

southern athiest. oh, honey
by d. e. fulford

Bruises, Birthmarks & Other Calamities
by Nadine Klassen

Wanted: Comedy, Addicts
by AR Dugan

They Curve Like Snakes
by David Alexander McFarland

the catalog of daily fears
by Beth Dufford

Shops Close Too Early
by Josh Feit

Vanity Unfair and Other Poems
by Robert Eugene Rubino

Destructive Heresies
by Milo E. Gorgevska

Bodies of Separation
by Chim Sher Ting

The Night with James Dean and Other Prose Poems
by Allison A. deFreese

About Time
by Julie Benesh

Quomodo probatur in conflatorio
by Nick Roberts

The Unempty Spaces Between
by Louis Efron

Cathexis Northwest Press

www.ingramcontent.com/pod-product-compliance
Lightning Source LLC
Chambersburg PA
CBHW050335120526
44592CB00014B/2194